TWO✕ISM

8th House Publishing
Montreal, Canada

A CIP catalogue of this book is available from
LIBRARIES AND ARCHIVES CANADA
CATALOGUING IN PUBLICATION

Serea, Claudia, author
Twoxism / poems by Claudia Serea; photos by Maria Haro
and collaborators — First edition

Contents: Sometimes I feel like a mechanic — The city pulls us apart —
We'll always have summer

ISBN 978-1-926716-53-4 (softcover)

I. Haro, Maria, 1970-, photographer II. Title. I II. Title: Twoism

PS3619.E73T86 2018   811'.6   C2018-906498-6

8th House Publishing
Montreal, Canada

TWOISM

Poems by Claudia Serea
Photos by Maria Haro

and collaborators

Contents

Part III: We'll always have summer

If there are junkyards in hell,
love is the dog that guards the gates.

—*Charles Bukowski,* Love Is a Dog From Hell

What is TWOXISM

Twoxism is a poem-photo collaboration project between two life-long friends: Maria Haro, a visual artist, and Claudia Serea, a poet.

Twoxism, an invented word for all things two, is about love, life, friendship, and relationships. *Twoxism* brings out the lyricism of urban photography and searches for beauty in unexpected places, looking at the mundane with redemptive eyes. It's a city love story, tender and gritty at the same time.

It all started in 2014 when Maria snapped some photos in New York City and posted them on Instagram. She noticed the objects on the city streets, the ones no one pays any attention to—trash cans, pipes, traffic cones—and wandered: *What if they mimic our existence? What if they are just like us? After all, we, the humans, created them.*

She noticed that many objects come in pairs, as if they wouldn't want to be alone. They endure together the hot sun, rain, sleet, and snow. They age together. So, she e-mailed her friend Claudia who wrote poems in response to the photographs. They posted the collaborations online in a blog format—and *Twoxism* was born.

But this is not an ordinary ekphrastic project. The photos don't act as mere prompts, but work with the poems as counterpoints. The blog's motto is *It takes two to tango—* and, as in the Argentinian tango, the poem-photo pair creates a push-pull tension between the visual and the verse. The poem only sometimes expresses the mood of the photo. Other times, it acts in contrast, offering a love note to balance the roughness of urban decay.

Like friendship, love, and life, these collaborations suggest the give and take of a tango and of a real relationship. They create their own relationships. They play against each other, meeting the rough with the smooth, the old with the new, sorrow with joy, and darkness with light.

Since 2015, the blog has built a strong audience of +7,500 with +15K page views and +40K impressions on Twitter and growing. Pages from the blog were widely shared on StumbleUpon (1,625 stumbles for the combo titled *Sometimes I feel like a mechanic* that opens the book). 33 poem-photo selections were turned into an art exhibition that opened in New York City in April 2017. And the story continues in book form today.

The book *Twoxism* picks up the love story theme and develops it further. Its three sections follow a couple's journey through the city, from falling in love, to breaking up, to finding love again in the end. New York City is their "stage" as well as another character in this story, with Madrid and Tokyo making cameo appearances.

We'd love to hear from you—so click, comment, and share. Follow us on Facebook and Instagram. See more photo-poem pairs at twoxism.com. Let us know about your own twoxisms, your own encounters with everyday objects and the stories or poems they bring to mind. It takes two to tango—but the more, the merrier.

I

Sometimes I feel like a

mechanic

Madrid, Spain.

Sometimes I feel like a mechanic

Sometimes I feel like a mechanic,
hammer and wrench
instead of hands,

fitting the small parts,
turning them this way
and that,
until they lock together,
tight,
teeth clenched.

I test the wheels,
try the belt,
turn the engine on
and off,
and on again,

listening to the wheezing,
the whirr,
until it works,
and the growl comes on,

and the propeller starts flipping
and swooshing,

and the shiny thing
lifts into the air
and flies into the world,

leaving me behind
with my greasy hands
and grimy nails,

grinning.

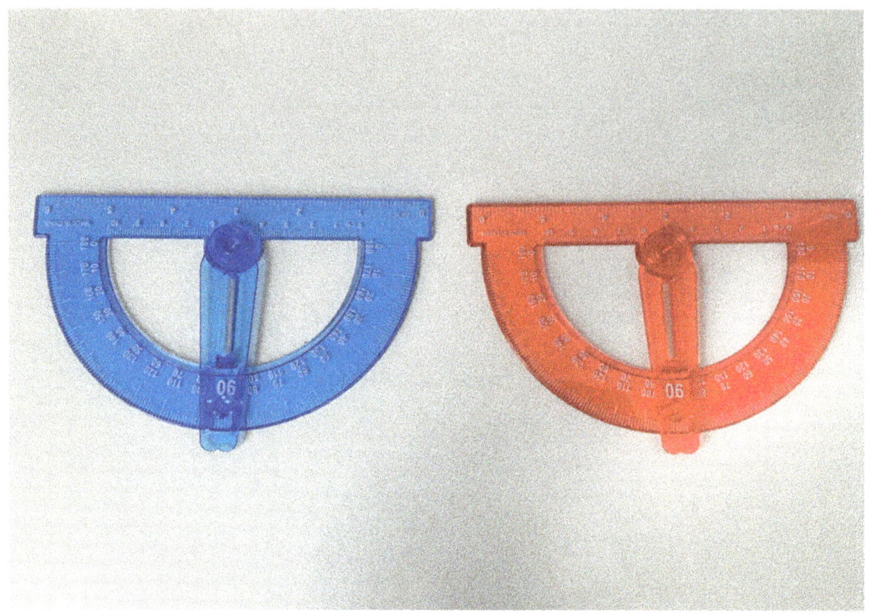

Long Island City, NY.

Red mountain, blue hill

This is goddess country,
the red mountain,
blue hill,
and the snowy valley
between them.

In front of it, love,
you're a child, a lover,
and a friend.

The child hides his fears
in the red mountain
and suckles at the blue hill breast.

The cartographer lover measures
the roundness of the blue hill,
the angles of the red mountain,
and carefully traces the map
of this woman land.

And the friend listens
to the blue hill breathing
and the heartbeat
under the red mountain:

Hear me, love.
I'm here.
I'm alive.

Why I love chocolate

Because it starts with a small white flower
in the *Theobroma cacao* tree
whose name means "food for the gods."

Because chocolate is old and well-traveled,
and cocoa beans were used as currency
by the Aztecs.

Because it comes from the plumed serpent,
Quetzalcoatl, a god cast away
for sharing chocolate with humans,

and shelling the cocoa beans from the pod
mimics removing human hearts
in sacrifice.

Because it's fermented, roasted, and bitter,
and, like life, can cover surprises
and liquor.

Because 50 million people around the world
depend on it.

Because it thins the blood
and soothes the mood.

Because Montezuma
and Casanova consumed it.

Because I grew up not having it,
wanting it,
and waiting for it in line for hours,
as if it were a holy relic.

Because it's forbidden.

Herald Square, NY.

Because it stands for love,
food for this goddess,

and blooms in my mouth,
a sweet dark flower.

Herald Square, NY.

A question for you

Tell me,
if I caught your shadow
and kissed it,

would you walk only
on the sunny side of the streets

so you wouldn't lose
my kiss?

Without a mouth

Without a mouth,
I'll kiss you with my silence.

Without hands, I'll caress you
with a sparrow.

I'll tie a rain cloud
with a ribbon

and float it to you
when you're bored.

We'll laugh at strangers
and their funny hair.

When everyone is gone,
we'll stick out light tongues
to the floors.

Tokyo, Japan.

42nd Street, New York City, NY.

In another subway life

Crooked,
aligned,

will we still be together
in another subway life?

Will you still love me?
Will you still want me

to refill your Metro Card,
to touch start

and begin?

TWO✕ISM

Calle de la Cruz, Madrid, Spain.

When I miss you

I put on my night cape
and step into your dream
as if it were a clothing store window
on Calle de La Cruz,

full of dressed or naked shadows,
lit by a single lamp.

I lie on the bed next to you
and cover you with kisses,
a field of red poppies.

By dawn, I'm gone.

Breeze for your sail

Tonight, the world is an abandoned lot
enclosed by chain link fences,
and us, trapped,

two helpless birds,
two fish caught in nets,
two knotted napkins.

But I'll say to you,
Hang on, love,
hang on.

Don't raise your white flags yet.
Don't surrender.

I'm sending you
a breeze for your sail,
sweet wind of faith.

I'll blow a lock of hair
off your pale forehead

and sing to you
from far away.

Don't give up, *mi amor*.

Together, we'll hang on
the wires of the world.

We'll billow, sway,
and flutter.

Soon, the fence will crumble
and we'll dance.

Long Island City, NY.

Madrid, Spain.

Love me

With gusts of wind through lace curtains
and white bed sheets,

love me with water, endless spring rain,
love me with chocolate and champagne,
fill bathtubs, tunnels, and pipes,

love me like fire, blindfolded and light,
like a rock concert in a burning library,

like a bullet train leaving the station
with cellos and violins—

love me like ghosts in the old palace,
with hammers and swords,

love me like war,
with dust, tanks, and humvees,

crunch me between your teeth
like a rose stem,

love me like a bargain,
like barter, give me your heart

and I'll give you rice
and a chicken for it,

love me like the sun loves the moon,
soup the spoon,
and cheesy pasta hugs the fork,

love me like a breeze in your hair,
love me like your breath,

like all life
and all death.

Madrid, Spain.

Cucarachas

Don't you wanna know
what these cockroaches have seen—

the turnips' breasts,
eggplants' shiny buttocks,

and us, making love
on the floor?

Tutti Matti Restaurant, Long Island City, NY.

Saturday night song

It's Saturday night in the city
with bars full of lovers
and poets drinking in the back rooms.

And the restaurants are full,
and the clubs pump, hot,
the music, loud,
the voices, louder,
hot, hot, damn hot,

and the streets burst
with laughter and love
full of young bodies,
full of love machines.

It's Saturday night.
We're gonna have some fun, baby.

All we need is the beat,
the boom,
so we can be it,
hot, hot, damn hot,
bi-bi-di-bing-bong-bang,

and the love machines blow hot air
from the cayenne moon.

It's Saturday night, baby.

Gimme your hot love,
hot, hot, damn hot.

I need it like air.

32

Korea Town, New York City, NY.

And that's how it happened

AHA! said the sidewalk,
finally understanding
what's happening.

HA! answered the trash.
I used to be a love note,
indecent, like a Kalashnikov
in a coffee shop.

I love you, said the wind,
picking up the trash
and lifting it

so the traffic light could read
the love note
and blush.

Red and white

Tonight I'll wear a red dress,
crimson heart on my sleeve,

pulsing,
like the meat thrown to lions.

Tonight, I'm a flame
in high heels,

a locked door
you'll open

with the purest
snow key.

Alicante, Spain.

47th Road, Long Island City, NY.

Snow

Snow falls everywhere all the time,
especially in far-away places,
like Eastern Europe,
Africa, or Thailand.

We trail the blizzard with us,
a cape covering continents.

Snow falls over the city,
over gray buildings, cars, and noise.

White noise,
snow falls between us,
curtains, walls,
and mountains fall.

Snow falls on your coat,
in your hair and eyelashes.

When we speak,
snowflakes get in our mouths.

It snows inside us, until
we fill with silence.

Now let's make snow angels
inside each other.

I love the way you sound

Love, crawl into my ear
and curl there,
in the dark.

Listen to the sounds
of my body,

the boom of the ocean
of blood.

Listen to the sounds
of the empty room.

Listen
to the sounds of falling snow.

Keep listening
to all the whispers
in the city.

Whisper to me, love.

Valdemoro, Madrid, Spain.

Long Island City, NY.

Christmas light

This Christmas, I wish for light
because light is the glue
that binds us
and pulls us through.

Light and love,
two moons swelling the tides,

two lit lamps
at the end of the street,

two huskies
pulling the sled of the heart
into the night.

II

The city pulls us apart

Herald Square, NY.

The space between

The space between the legs
walking the space between

me and you, two dark buildings
with white shirts hanging

on the clotheslines between us,
two trees on a hill

with or without a hammock in the space
between the branches full of wind,

with or without a mockingbird
in the space between

the arms, with or without embrace
in the space between breaths,

the space between lips,
between teeth and tongue,

between skin and blade,
between life and death.

About languages

In what language
does the house painter paint?

Does the wind in Chile
speak Spanish to the trees?

Do the gulls over the Hudson River cry
Whitman's verse?

And what about
the Statue of Liberty?

In what language does she
keep silent?

East Village, New York City, NY.

What you seek seeks you

What you seek is seeking you
—Rumi

If you're a hawk, love,
you wear a hood,

and I'm the leather glove
on which you land.

Love, if you're a twig nest,
I'm the abandoned egg.

In spring, my sparrow pain will hatch,
meet other sparrows

chatting in the trees
and pecking crumbs.

If you're a garden, love,
I'm your sweet soil,

cleaved and fertile,
teeming with red worms.

From my manure heart,
small flowers grow,

their roots reaching
for darkness.

Rutherford, NJ.

Ode to the traffic lights

The city wears you
as jeweled pins.

Must be nice to have so many obey
your commands,

to allow, or not allow,
the right of way.

O traffic lights,
most useful machines
watching us from above
with your Cyclops red eyes,

you don't care
if someone's in a hurry,
if anyone misses the plane,
or if I'm late to pick up my daughter
from school.

In the strongest storm, you sway
at the crossroads
and attempt to tell the wind
to stop.

Unfazed,
even after a robbery late at night,
you still change your light to green,
letting the thief get away.

Don't walk, you order me,
and give me a minute to look up
at the parallel movie of the sky,

and think about the traffic lights
from all the cities in the world,
and their quiet, benevolent
dictatorship.

Atocha, Madrid, Spain.

Walk, you say next—
and millions of us do,
crossing the streets, thoughtless,

rhythmically flowing
like blood cells
in the city's veins.

Madrid, Spain.

Love / Hate

This is the god with two faces
I carry engraved in skin and bone,

two sides of the same coin
tossed up and called
in mid-air.

My good,
my evil,

heads or tails.

This time,
in love we trust.

Halloween style

A city rat will be
your savvy driver,
hair slicked,
sunglasses on,
impeccable in his gray uniform
with epaulets.

He'll open the door
of the custard-colored limo,
and you'll step out:
carrot-pointed
Balenciaga shoes,
saffron and wine
Armani coat,
sunflower silk
Vera Wang dress,
and a candy corn necklace
from Van Cleef & Arpels.

No mask,
just Gucci shades,
and, underneath it all, the scent
of Coco Mademoiselle.

You'll go up to the ballroom
where you'll meet your Arab prince.

And you'll dance
among presidents and movie stars
dressed as themselves.

At midnight, all will go away:

SOHO, New York City, NY.

the limousine,
the driver,
the prince,
the tricks and treats.

You'll be back on 5th Avenue,
looking in the window
at the pumpkin handbag
from Louis Vuitton.

Borden Avenue, Long Island City, NY.

Love is not a microphone

After the party,
when everyone goes home,

this is what's left:

a tangle of beads,
days in a string of broken pearls
with an ampersand
at the end.

The opposite of two
is one.

The antonym of love
is not hate,

but alone.

In a jazz bar in the East Village

I could peek through
the closed door
between the kitchen
and the hallway,

between light and dark,
boiling hot
and cutting cold,

yelling loud
and quiet moan,

between sin
and sainthood.

On Friday night,
in a jazz bar in the East Village,
on my way to the bathroom,

I peeked through the door
between heaven and hell.

Jules' Live Jazz. East Village, New York City, NY.

I go to the kitchen and turn on the faucet

Pain gushes out,
filtered,
clean,
straight from the treatment plant.

It has a vague scent of chlorine.

I wait for the steady flow,
pour it into a cup,
drink it,

sprinkle the rest of it
on my windowsill flowers.

The other faucet is broken—
no joy to do the dishes.

Pain runs down the steel sink drain,
plentiful,
clear.

I wash my hands in it,
splash some on my face,
and turn off the faucet.

Under the city,
the pipes moan slightly.

Long Island City, NY.

Fuencarral, Madrid, Spain.

La maté por que era mía

The smile was not hers.
It was mine.

Mine,
the curls of her hair,

her hands,
her breasts,

her delicate feet,
all mine.

The way she moved,
she danced,

she breathed,
mine.

Mine.

Nothing was hers.

Not even the small,
red painted toes.

'O'

'O'.'O'.'O'.'O'.'O'.'O'.'O'.'O'.'O'.'O'.
'O'.'O'.'O'.'O'.'O'.'O'.'O'.'O'.'O'.'O'.
'O'.'O'.'O'.'O'.'O'.'O'.'O'.'O'.'O'.'O'.
'O'.'O'.'O'.'O'.'O'.'O'.'O'.'O'.'O'.'O'.
'O'.'O'.'O'.'O'.'O'.'O'.'O'.'O'.'O'.'O'.
'O'.'O'.'O'.'O'.'O'.'O'.'O'.'O'.'O'.'O'.

'O'.'O'.'O'.'O'.'O'.'O'.'O'.'O'.'O'.'O'.
'O'.'O'.'O'.'O'.'O'.'O'.'O'.'O'.'O'.'O'.
'O'.'O'.'O'.'O'.'O'.'O'.'O'.'O'.'O'.'O'.
'O'.'O'.'O'.'O'.'O'.'O'.'O'.'O'.'O'.'O'.
'O'.'O'.'O'.'O'.'O'.'O'.'O'.'O'.'O'.'O'.
'O'.'O'.'O'.'O'.'O'.'O'.'O'.'O'.'O'.'O'.

New York City, NY.

Mourning coffee

For the 200 jumpers from the
WTC Towers on 9/11/2001

On one side,
the roar of the flames,
the unbearable hot
deathly mouth.

On the other side,
fresh air.

You couldn't breathe,
and there was the escape:

bright sun,
light wind,
and silence.

An angel without wings,
you chose
to step into the void.

It must have felt like flying,
a thing of beauty,
the body's delicate
ten seconds ballet,

feet apart,
knees bent,
straight arms
at high speed.

And you evaporated
into the breeze.

Manhattan Mall, New York City, NY.

Years later,
nobody claims your name,
the one scribbled by the barista
on the coffee cup
you didn't drink.

Long Island City, NY.

Two closed doors

Tell me, which door leads to the past?
The other, to the future?

Which one is jail?
Which one is home?

And which one I can open
with my heart key?

Which one is love? And hate?
Which one is sorrow?

And behind which one will you wait,
eating a slice of bread,

flipping the channels,
growing a beard?

Behind which door are we together?
Behind which ones, apart?

The city pulls us apart

With the outstretched arms
of the mannequins at Macy's,
with 34th Street
and 7th Ave,

with intersections
and millipedes
of feet on sidewalks,

the city pulls us apart.

It forks ahead
and zips up on our heels.

We join in bedrooms,
in restaurants and bars,
in The New Yorker
and The Hound,

and part in Bloomingdale's
and in Penn Station,

come back together
in cinemas and Bryant Park,

and step away at work,
in public bathrooms,
on trains, further away,
in Lincoln Tunnel,
and more work.

It's not your fault,
or mine
that JFK pulls us apart,
that life pulls us apart.

New York City, NY.

And then we're back again
on Skype.

I have to go now, bye.

The city pulls us apart,
the city pulls us,
the city pulls.

Vernon Boulevard, Long Island City, NY.

High stakes entertainment

When all of this is over,
we'll have invented a new game,
the American roulette.

All is fair in love and war.

So pass the popcorn,
the wine,
lots of wine,
and the remote.

In the dark museum of your body

The smoke art costs
a few bucks.

Here's the charred throat,
the flaky lungs covered in soot,

and the coiled monster saying
you're gonna die soon enough.

The custodian sleeps in a corner,
a newspaper over his head.

But in the last room,
a small bird still sings

and all you need to do
is open a window

and let the fresh air
and sunshine rush in.

Valdemoro, Madrid, Spain.

III

We'll always have
summer

Herald Square, New York City, NY.

Parallel heavens

Doors closed,
lawns freshly mowed,
the heavens line up,
a row of suburban houses
on a quiet street.

I imagine mine painted white,
silent and sleepy,
a provincial art museum
where all the angels have been assigned
to perpetual paperwork.

One can't even think
to jump from one heaven
into another
without wings,
or breaking a bone.

And each heaven
has its own way to get to it
on parallel stairways,
steps, and ladders.

The old man sets the ladders against the walls,
side by side.

From here,
we can only go up.

The tree in winter

Don't think of me as naked,
shivering in the cold wind.

Don't think I'm dead,
or worse.

Don't pity me,

for you don't know
resistance.

My strength is underground,
in the country of bones
and red worms,

where flags fly
upside down.

When the wind bends
my branches,
listen
for battle noise,

the rising, sprawling
riot of the roots:

an army,
gathering.

Herald Square, New York City, NY.

Ode to the warrior woman

Beautiful woman,
the world is still cruel and wild.
Bring out the thunderbolts
and don't be afraid of the fight.

Put on your lipstick
and pull up your boots.
Grab your sword
and slay the dragons on your way to work.

Walk in knee-high blood
on 7th Avenue
and don't let anyone see the quiver
in your heart.

Be kind and smile.
Don't let them see that you're hurt.

Sharpen your talons,
merciless bird.

Woman, you da man,
the man's womb,
you da bomb!

Galaxies explode from your sex!
Milky Way swirls
and pours
out of your breasts.

Tell the little girl inside you to hush.

Swing the bow on your back
and spread your eagle wings.

There is so much to fight for,
so much to do.

Put on your lipstick, girl.
The world is waiting for you.

Sister, little sister

Sister, little sister,
teach me how
to lean into the breeze
and part it
with my hands.

How will I find
the truth about myself
and glide
on sandpaper highways?

Sister,
skateboard sister,
show me how
I can ignore my tears
and scraped knees.

When no one's around,
how can I carve my name
with the kick flip
and the skid
into the long slide?

Will I die today?

Or will I pick up
my board and skate
my life away?

P.S. 78, Long Island City, NY.

Long Island City, NY.

Waxing crescent

The moon still lights the treetops tonight,
bitten by darkness,

and I know its phases wouldn't exist
without the shadow,

the way joy wouldn't be
without sorrow

and apple wedges
without the knife.

So cut me with your bad news, world,
all you want.

It will only shape
my hope.

Do you miss my hands?

I miss you, gloves,
your softness on my skin,
your tightly-sewn friendship.

Do you miss my hands, too?

You were a gift from my lover
who wanted to hold my hand
from far away.

I wonder where I lost you,
and, if you're still together, a pair,
or separated in despair.

I wonder if you're somewhere on the sidewalk,
stepped-on by passers-by,
pointing to them the north-south-east-west,
or directing traffic
in the middle of the street,

or hanging out
at the lost-and-found
with the umbrellas and the phones,
enjoying your freedom.

Maybe a homeless man will pick you up,
and you'll warm his knotty hands.

Or maybe a boy will find you
and use you to make hands
for the snowman he's building
in his yard.

He'll place you at the ends of two twigs
stuck in the round body,
and you'll point again to houses,
squirrels, and cars.

Long Island City, NY.

And you'll survive the snowman.

In spring, maybe a bird will line its nest
with what's left of you

and the chicks' warmth will remind you
of my hands.

Tumbada

In protest, we fall to the ground.

Maimed by betrayal,
tired, dented, used,
and discarded by the curb,

I can't offer you more
than this poem.

Long after the crowds are gone,
we still hold high our flags,
proud of what we stood for.

Tumbled,
but not defeated.

Borden Avenue, Long Island City, NY.

P.S. 141, Astoria, Queens, NY.

A chair is just a chair

It's the hot chair you sit on
in the middle of the highway
that has become your life,
where trucks and cars swoosh by,
barely missing you.

It's the school chair
you sat on as a child,
still as a statue,
and flew over rooftops, reading
a burning book.

It's the cool chair on the ocean floor
where you sit and sip tea
your hair floating around your face
and sharks swim by, indifferent.

It's the chair in the doctor's office
where you sit, holding the hand
of your best friend,
waiting for the test results.

And everyone else admires
how calm you are
and how serene you sit
on your chair on the moon
and peel an orange.

How do the birds know when it's time to fly?

They must feel a restlessness,
or a clock
striking in their brain,

an itch,
or a longing
in the bones.

Or maybe the roads are calling,
unfolding ahead,

new balconies of the city,
glimmering windows
and highways of air.

That's when I have to say goodbye
to my friends
of the same feather

and prepare to travel light,
with only love
as carry-on.

Then, without thinking too much,
the leap:

the push
off the ledge,
a flap or two.

I lean my chest against the wind
and glide.

The current pours
and lifts me up, up,
so I can see everything.

Farewell, past.

Herald Square, New York City, NY.

Wishes for a Star Wars fan

May the light be with you,
the sun on the sidewalk where you camped,

and the moon, the stars, and supernovas
in a galaxy far, far away.

May the universe be with you.

And luck, and kindness,
money, and good teeth.

And love, let's not forget love.
May love be always with you.

May George Lucas be with you,
and Disney, and Harrison Ford.
And, when you need it most,

may Chewbacca come to the rescue.

May you always carry a light saber of courage.

And may you always care,
and save the world.

May laughter and excitement be with you,
and an ice-cold Coke.

May gravity keep you grounded,
and happiness make you float.

May the odds be always in your favor—
wait, wrong movie, scratch that.

May wisdom be with you
and Obi-Wan Kenobi.

Long Island City, NY.

And may you find the secrets
and hidden treasures you're searching for,
but leave some mysteries unsolved.
May the light be with you, my friend.

And the force,
always the force.

House hunting on Sundays

We counted all the city windows
and all the lights.

A goldfish swam across the sky,
and granted us three wishes.

We wished to see the stars,
and we moved from the city.

We wished for an orchestra
to play in the background
when we were counting stars,

and we got crickets.

At dawn, we wished to be
forever young.

And we were.

Long Island City, NY.

Art study

The bus enters a pencil drawing,
passes a bridge over a smudge.

Squares, houses, triangles, roofs,
trees of charcoal,

the spatter of leaves and paints
over suburbia,

and your face, a sketch
barely reflected in the window.

We sit in the back: white teeth, black hands,
gray criss-cross of silence.

We pass from one frame
to another, in darkness.

It rains clear yellow, fall's color,
the color of death.

Embraced, we walk on alleys of air.
We are alive.

Tokyo, Japan.

Long Island City, NY.

We'll always have summer

We'll always have potholes,
dirt, and rust.

At some point,
my goddess wings will crumble.

Your vinyl seat
will tear apart.

Grass and moss will grow
through our missing spokes.

Duct-taped,
flat-tired,
paint chipped,

we'll go through sun
and rain
and piles of snow,
thieves' hands,
and pigeon shit.

Around us, the city will rise and fall
in screeching tides,

but we'll always have the summer.

And the summer after that.

Ode to beer

Beer the color of summer,
dusk-colored beer
with golden feet and foamy beard,

blue-collared beer,
honest and filling,
loud, and gregarious, and cool,

here's to you.

I love you more than wine
because you're cold and clear,
waiting on ice on a hot day
with or without shade,
with or without a lime,
or a beach.

Because wine is pretentious
and water too plain,
and you're humble,
and taste of grain.

Because nobody writes you odes
although you buzz,
pop, and fizzle,
and rise from yeast like life.

Because your name is simple.

Because you hail from Mesopotamia
where Gilgamesh drank you
with Enkidu.

Because you're best sipped
in the haunts of the Old City,
on a terrace in Bucharest
or Madrid,
with a brother or best friend.

Penn Station, New York City, NY.

Here's to you, old god
who takes the tiredness away
after a long day walking,
who takes the years
we've been apart away,

and makes us young,
laughing,
happy again.

How we escaped

We rode our orange scooters
into the sunset.

There were fires burning
and gangs fighting
on the outskirts of the city,

but we zoomed by.

The days were blue blurs.
The nights were black.

The golden woods didn't say anything.

The golden woods were a birdcage
with its door open

and a red bird
deep inside,

singing.

Long Island City, NY.

Madrid, Spain.

Andrés asked the love of his life to marry him

And she said yes.
How the hell

I ever thought I could go on
living alone? he asked himself.

Quiet and old-fashioned,
love fell over them, simple

like the sun through the window,
warming their toes

and her shapely body
designed in Toledo, OH.

Drink Me, she said,
in her bubbly, sweet voice.

Yes-yes-yes, Andrés nodded,
a glint in his eyes.

After that, they sat in silence,
smiling.

A sparrow took the news
to the sky.

Acknowledgments

Grateful acknowledgment is made to the editors of the
following journals and anthologies where some of these
poems first appeared, sometimes in earlier versions: *Ascent,
The Broome Review, The Brownstone Poets Anthology,
Gravel, Grey Sparrow Journal, Lévure Litteraire,
Live Encounters, Poetry Riot, Radius: Poetry from the
Center to the Edge, RWB Poem of the Week 2,* and
The Red Wheelbarrow.

The poems *And That's How It Happened, The City Pulls
Us Apart, Waxing Crescent, The Tree in Winter,* and
High Stakes Entertainment were set to music for choir by
composer Theo Chandler. Hats off to Theo.

The poems *Snow* and *Christmas Light* were produced as
video poems in 2018 by Paul Broderick. Many thanks, Paul.

33 poem-photo selections were turned into the *Twoxism* art
exhibition that opened in New York City in April 2017.
Our gratitude to Rich Levy for organizing this event.

Grateful acknowledgment is made to the following
photographer friends who contributed to this project:

Koldo Miren Guinea Herran for the photos on the cover and on
pages **10, 26, 28, 51,** and **62**

Luis Mendo for the photos on pages **19** and **101**

Raquel Haro for the photo on page **39**

Elliott Jover for the photo on page **97**

More at **www.twoxism.com**

About the authors and collaborators

Claudia Serea is an award-winning Romanian-born poet whose
poems and translations appeared in *Field, New Letters, Gravel,
Prairie Schooner, RHINO, The Malahat Review,* and elsewhere.
She is the author of four other poetry collections, most recently
Nothing Important Happened Today (Broadstone Books, 2016).
Serea co-hosts The Williams Readings in Rutherford, NJ, and
she is a founding editor of National Translation Month.

Maria Haro grew up in Madrid, Spain, where she studied
fine arts and graphic design. She graduated from the School
of Graphic Communications and moved to New York City in
1994. She has won several global awards as a Creative Director
in pharma advertising. She collaborates with other artists on
projects that inspire her. You can find her photos on Instagram.

Koldo Miren Guinea Herran is a Spanish designer and illustrator
with editorial work published in various Spanish magazines.
He is represented by Fillin Global, and you can see his latest
illustrations here: http://www.fillinglobal.com/#/new-gallery-2/.

After a successful career as creative director in Amsterdam,
Luis Mendo moved to Tokyo where he works as a drawing
artist. He is represented by Fillin Global, and you can see his
work on the Fillin web site and at luismendo.com.

Raquel Haro is a Spanish designer, illustrator, and tattoo
artist who studied art and design in Madrid and loves fashion
illustration and mixed media. You can see her work on the Fillin
Global web site: http://www.fillinglobal.com/#/raquel-haro/.

Elliot Jover is a senior at High School of Art and Design in
New York City and loves the arts, design, photography, soccer,
and videogames. You can find his photos on Instagram.